T0286819

URBAN BUSES IN NORTHERN ENGLAND: A SECOND VIEW

PETER TUCKER

AMBERLEY

At Cheetham, Go North West No. 69204, a Wright-bodied Volvo B7RLE, traverses Cheetham Hill Road, Manchester, during December 2021.

The book is dedicated to the late Revd John Campbell of Hexham.

Front cover: Stagecoach No. 27180 is an Alexander Dennis Enviro300 pictured on 31 August 2021 at Albert Road, Middlesbrough.

Back cover: Preston Bus No. 20158 at Tudor Avenue, Farringdon Park, on a dismal 29 October 2021.

First published 2023

Amberley Publishing
The Hill, Stroud
Gloucestershire, GL5 4EP

www.amberley-books.com

Copyright © Peter Tucker, 2023

The right of Peter Tucker to be identified as the Author of this work has been asserted in accordance with the Copyrights, Designs and Patents Act 1988.

ISBN 978 1 3981 1347 3 (print)
ISBN 978 1 3981 1348 0 (ebook)

All rights reserved. No part of this book may be reprinted or reproduced or utilised in any form or by any electronic, mechanical or other means, now known or hereafter invented, including photocopying and recording, or in any information storage or retrieval system, without the permission in writing from the Publishers.

British Library Cataloguing in Publication Data.
A catalogue record for this book is available from the British Library.

Origination by Amberley Publishing.
Printed in the UK.

Introduction

In this edition of *Urban Buses*, I aim to give a broad panorama of the current bus scene in northern England. The book covers the area from the English border down to the metropolitan counties of Greater Manchester, Merseyside and South Yorkshire. Most of North Yorkshire and all of East Yorkshire are excluded in this edition, although York, which was historically outside the 'Ridings', is included. Cumbria and Northumberland receive limited coverage due to their largely rural nature. To make up for the comparative neglect of the north-west in the previous publication, there is a greater focus on Lancashire and Merseyside. I also include a photograph from Derbyshire, plus a selection from Cheshire East – those parts which are more or less extensions of Greater Manchester.

The earliest photographs are from 1993 when I was a teenager, armed with a no-frills but reliable Samsung camera. The most recent are from 2021 and January 2022. Great changes have taken place in the interim. Bus stations have been rebuilt; buses are equipped with features undreamt of in the past such as Wi-Fi and cashless payment. Towns and cities have evolved – most are cleaner but not necessarily more attractive. Some are more diverse, others have more students and nearly all face challenges. This is not a book about bus types, engines and companies per se; rather it is a visual and historic record for future generations. Many of the pictures attempt to show buses in their environment such as bus stations, depots, key arterial routes or suburbs.

As can be expected it is difficult to include all the urban areas of northern England. Some places I have never visited such as Chorley and Southport, while others I never seem to have a camera on me – Hyde, Rawtenstall and Peterlee. So apologies to: Altrincham, Bacup, Chorley, East Yorkshire, Horbury, Penistone, Peterlee, Scarborough, Selby, Tynemouth, Workington and elsewhere for missing you out. On the other hand, this book does include somewhat underrepresented places such as Billingham, Farnworth, Nelson, Pontefract, South Bank, Speke and elsewhere.

I hope you enjoy this collection of photographs of buses in the urban areas of northern England. The book will be interesting to return too in several decades time – or so I hope! Those who would like to know more about buses themselves and bus operators are recommended to read the excellent *Bus Handbook* series or the various bus magazines such as *Buses*, available in newsagents. There are also numerous websites and of course the PSV Circle.

I would like to thank Thomas Anthony for proofreading the text, plus Sister Margaret Atkins and Alice for their support. A special thank you to Kevin Lane and the late T. W. Moore, artists whose photographs really elevate bus photography to an artistic level! Finally, any errors in this book are mine.

All photographs are by the author unless otherwise stated.

Darlington Transport No. 70 was one of four Leyland Leopards with unique Duple Dominant bodywork delivered in 1976. Originally fitted with dual-doors, these buses featured high-backed seats and steep steps, making access particularly difficult for elderly passengers. No. 70 was pictured at The Dolphin Centre, Darlington, in February 1993.

Yorkshire Rider purchased York City & District in 1990, branding the fleet as Rider York. The stylish lines of No. 1332, a former West Yorkshire Road Car Leyland National 2, were photographed from the top-deck of an Atlantean open-topper in April 1993. The brutal post-war building on the right represents one of the many styles and periods of architecture in York.

Perhaps the bus most associated with Newcastle-upon-Tyne until the 1990s was the Alexander-bodied Leyland Atlantean. Busways No. 319 was new to predecessor Tyne & Wear PTE and carries the elegant, Alexander AL-type bodywork. Tyne & Wear PTE also had Atlanteans bodied by MCW (later transferred to Northern), plus a notoriously ungainly batch by Willowbrook, used mainly at Sunderland. No. 319 was photographed at Newgate Street, Newcastle-upon-Tyne, during July 1994.

At Otley, Yorkshire Rider Bradford's No. 5515 looks very smart in West Yorkshire Road Car heritage livery. D515 HUB is a rare Leyland Olympian/Optare combination new in 1987. Optare were formed in 1985 from the ashes of Charles Henry Roe, the Leeds-based bodybuilder closed by Leyland in 1984. Subsequent Optare designs would include the City Pacer and Delta.

Northumbria inherited numerous dual-purpose Leyland Leopards from United in 1986. No. 204 was one of five 1977–78 Leopards to be rebuilt by Hestair Duple in 1987, the original bodies being in unsatisfactory condition due to corrosion and questionable build quality. The Duple 320 bodies constructed for Northumbria were notoriously cramped and uncomfortable on long journeys. No. 204 speeds out of Amble, Northumberland on the limited stop X18 to Newcastle.

Stanley is a frequently windswept place in a part of County Durham once dominated by coal mining. Photographed leaving the now closed bus station is Northern's sleek DAF SB220/Optare Delta complete with DAF 11.6-litre engine. Other operators of the impressive Optare Delta included Blackpool, Crosville Cymru, East Kent, TMS and United Automobile Services.

Keighley & District was formed from part of the privatised West Yorkshire Road Car Company. Operations were centred on Keighley and served destinations as diverse as Bradford, Grassington, Haworth, Ilkley, Skipton and Wetherby. Representing the mid-1990s livery is Leyland Olympian/ ECW No. 373, new in 1985 and photographed at St Peter's Street, Leeds, during March 1995. The notorious Quarry Hill Flats once dominated this part of Leeds. Completed in 1941, they housed over 3,200 people and were inspired by municipal schemes in Berlin and Vienna.

The late Howard Keel was due to perform at St George's Hall, Bradford, the distinctive building on the right of this April 1995 picture. Heading towards Bradford Interchange, No. 6228 already has the destination set for the return journey to Leeds. Yorkshire Rider was the successor to West Yorkshire PTE, which had been formed in 1974 to take over the running of the region's municipal operators, including Bradford City Transport.

In 1995 United's operating territory still included a large portion of rural North Yorkshire. Services served everywhere from Catterick Garrison to Keld, Leyburn, Masham, Ripon and York. There was still a joint service with Harrogate & District linking Ripon and Leeds via the A61. At Knaresborough, United No. 255, a Leyland Olympian/ECW combination, was pictured working the Ripon to Harrogate service on 6 May 1995.

Having favoured the well-proven Leyland Leopard for many years, Pennine of Gargrave purchased several Leyland Nationals in the 1990s. An odd choice perhaps, given the Nationals poor reputation for engine thirst, toxic fumes and indifferent reliability. LN8, a type B variant, had some advantages over the Leopard, notably a lower step entrance and a solid unitary construction. New to Alexander Midland as OLS 809T in 1978, she was photographed at Skipton, a town close to the Lancashire and West Yorkshire boundary.

Leyland Olympian/Alexander No. 5218 illustrates the Yorkshire Rider group in transition. The then new Bradford Traveller identity has been applied over Yorkshire Rider livery heralding a rebrand of the fleet. The bus was later painted in the smart Bradford Traveller blue, a nostalgic nod to Bradford City Transport. Harrogate, 1 July 1996.

Bradford Interchange was opened in March 1977 by West Yorkshire PTE. Designed to incorporate bus, rail and taxi facilities, plus an underground bus depot, the project was ultimately defeated by falling passenger numbers and high maintenance costs. An interesting concept and structure, the building was over-engineered and too far away from the main shopping area. The hilly climb up Bridge Street was an inconvenience for the elderly despite the Shop Hopper service. Pictured at the Interchange on 9 July 1996 are various Leyland Olympians, a Leyland Atlantean, Volvo Ailsa and B10M and an unidentified member of the Yorkshire Woollen fleet. Nearest the camera is Olympian No. 5204, an Alexander-bodied Leyland Olympian working out to Dewsbury.

York railway station was built outside the historic city walls and was sited close to a Roman burial ground. Glenn Line (Glenn Coaches) of Wiggington were operating this smart Leyland National, new in 1978, to Cymru Cenedlaethol, National Welsh to English speakers. She came via Potteries (PMT) of Stoke-on-Trent in 1995 and was photographed during the summer of 1996.

Representing contrasting styles of Roe bodywork are Leyland Atlanteans No. 6361 and No. 6015. New in December 1981 and October 1974 respectively, they are shown in the cavernous surroundings of Bradford Interchange on 9 July 1996. The design of Bradford Interchange was commended in 1978 by the *Financial Times* Industrial Architecture Award. Little of the complex survives today.

Representing Huddersfield heritage livery is Yorkshire Rider No. 6299, one of many Roe-bodied Leyland Atlanteans then in the fleet. She was about to leave Huddersfield for the intriguingly named Marsden Hard End, high up in the Pennine Hills towards Greater Manchester. Many routes in the Huddersfield area operate around hilly suburbs and satellite villages such as Golcar. Famous people from Huddersfield include James Mason and politicians Harold Wilson and Trevor O'Clochartaigh.

The gargantuan Bradford Interchange was being reconstructed in 1997 – twenty years after its opening. A large section to the south had been removed as can be seen in this 23 May photograph. Yorkshire Woollen No. 564, a Leyland Olympian/ECW, and a Yorkshire Traction Scania K113CB/Plaxton Paramount 3500 III, attired in National Express livery, are seen on layover. The post-war architecture in the background has been compared to designs in the Communist Eastern Bloc, being reminiscent of Tolyatti and Saratov.

Burnley & Pendle was formed in 1974 as the new name for the Burnley, Colne and Nelson Joint Transport Committee, which had been formed in 1933. Leaving the brutal but functional bus station at Nelson, Stagecoach Burnley & Pendle No. 424 heads north to Barnoldswick. The bus is a Volvo B10M-50/East Lancashire combination new in 1992. Stagecoach acquired Burnley & Pendle in stages during 1996–97 before selling its entire east Lancashire operations to Blazefield in 2001.

LN6 is a Leyland National 2, Series B, in the Pennine of Gargrave fleet. New in 1980 to West Yorkshire Road Car as PWY 583W, she was photographed at Burnley in 1998. Burnley nestles close to the Pennines and Pendle Hill – sublime scenery is never far away. Granted a market charter in 1293, Burnley's growth was due to the expansion of the local cotton and coal mining industries. A considerable part of Burnley was redeveloped from the 1960s, changing the character of the town centre forever.

Guisborough is a former mining town at the foot of the Cleveland Hills and North York Moors National Park. With a historic priory, verdant green hills and easy access to Teesside, the town is popular with commuters. Tees & District No. 3730 was inherited from United and is seen on a busy market day in April 1998.

Handsome dual-purpose buses were the batch of Duple-bodied Leyland Tigers delivered to West Yorkshire PTE in 1983–84. No. 1669, seen here at Halifax, provided a comfortable journey for the scenic run to Burnley via Mytholmroyd, Hebden Bridge and Todmorden. Over the centuries, the scenic but now semi-industrial Upper Calder Valley has suffered severe flooding, the first recorded deluge occurring in 1615.

Barnard Castle is popular with spin-doctors keen to test their ocular skills, especially during pandemics. Back in August 1998, Go Northern was operating No. 3491, a 1980 MCW Metrobus on the scenic service between 'Barney' and Bishop Auckland. New to Northern under NBC auspices, No. 3491 was photographed in OK Travel livery but with Go Northern branding, following the takeover of the Bishop Auckland firm in March 1995.

Yarm was originally in the North Riding of Yorkshire. Once a port on the River Tees, for a period it ranked ahead of Stockton-on-Tees in importance and trade. Today, it is thriving commuter town of considerable charm and affluence. By the old town hall and on the partly cobbled High Street is Tees & District No. 3740, a Leyland National 2, new to East Yorkshire in 1980. Yarm, August 1998.

The Leyland National 2 constituted a key part of the Yorkshire Traction fleet in the 1990s. No. 263 was new in 1982 and was pictured at Huddersfield bound for Clayton West. The National 2 is generally better regarded than the earlier version, production beginning in 1979 and ending in 1985.

The south end of the half-mile-long High Street at Stockton-on-Tees was considerably rebuilt in the early 1970s. The ungainly Swallow Hotel and Castlegate Centre on the left were demolished in stages from August 2022 as part of the Stockton Waterfront development. Passing Boots, Go North East No. 3668, a Leyland Olympian/ECW combination, heads north for Newcastle upon Tyne in June 1999.

The 8 July 1999 was a drab and overcast day in the seaside resort of Redcar. The subject of this picture, a Leyland Olympian, is overshadowed by a County tractor used by fishermen on the Redcar's broad and sandy beach. Historically a Yorkshire town, Redcar was traditionally United territory with services extending to Loftus, Middlesbrough, Stokesley, Stockton-on-Tees and Yarm.

KPJ 252W is Roe-bodied Leyland Atlantean, new to London Country in November 1980. Photographed in the ownership of Crossroads Coaches, she was off the road by 1 April 2001. Here, she leads a convoy of school buses out of St Leonard's Roman Catholic School, Durham, during June 2000.

Representing corporate First livery is No. 3015, a Volvo B6/Wright combination working the 513 to Mixenden. Bringing up the rear, in the short-lived Calderline livery, is former London Transport MCW Metrobus No. 7629. Halifax is the chief town of Calderdale, a borough that includes Brighouse, Elland, Hebden Bridge, Sowerby Bridge and Todmorden. Hills, mills and moors form the typical Calderdale landscape. Taken September 2001.

Representing the then current Stagecoach livery is MKO2 EGD, a Dennis Trident/Alexander ALX400 bound for Flixton in the Trafford district of Greater Manchester. At the rear, in the earlier Stagecoach colour scheme, is C226 ENE, a Leyland Olympian/Northern Counties combination working service 101 to Wythenshawe. Wythenshawe, formerly in Cheshire, was built as a large overspill settlement by Manchester Corporation to house families moved from slum clearance areas in the city – notably Ancoats and Hulme. The location is Piccadilly, Manchester, on 1 May 2002.

Although Cleveland Transit never purchased the Leyland National, they did order its successor, the Leyland Lynx. Thirty-one Lynxes were bought new by Transit, with more used examples added by Stagecoach. Photographed at Station Road, Billingham, an unidentified Leyland Lynx works service 52 to Stockton-on-Tees with a meagre number of passengers in early 2003.

A rear view picture of First Bradford No. 1076 working up the steep Carr Lane at Wrose. The ascent did not provide much of a challenge for the Volvo B10BLE as it left Shipley during April 2003.

On 20 February 2006, a Go North East Volvo B10BLE/Wright combination approaches Gateshead at Old Durham Road, Deckham. In the distance, the brutal post-war development of Gateshead dominates the scene, including the maligned Trinity Square multistorey car park development. The building featured in several memorable scenes of *Get Carter*, made in 1970 around Tyneside, County Durham and Blyth. The film released in 1971 by MGM has become a cult favourite, after decidedly mixed reviews on release.

Holmfirth is well known as the setting of the BBC comedy *Last of the Summer Wine*. With a backdrop typical of the area – solid stone-built properties and steep streets – Stott's Optare Solo works the Royds Avenue circular in October 2010. Holmfirth is in the Kirklees district of West Yorkshire and is situated close to the Peak District National Park.

In October 2018 an unfortunate National Express driver must have taken a wrong turn at Manchester Road, Wilmslow – he was probably trying to reach Manchester Airport or the A34. Heading towards Styal on a totally unsuitable road, the coach was unable to clear the hump at Linney's Bridge, Wilmslow. Forced into a complex manoeuvre, the back axle became stuck on a slippery embankment. Thankfully after much stress and mathematical skill the coach was extricated. I offered my services but they were politely declined!

Photographed at Newhey (New Hey on some maps) is First Manchester No. 33678, an Alexander Dennis Enviro400. Newhey is a village in the metropolitan borough of Rochdale, separated from Milnrow by the thunderous M62 motorway, the highest motorway in England. Rochdale Corporation was merged into SELNEC PTE (South East Lancashire North East Cheshire) on 1 November 1969. Greater Manchester PTE replaced SELNEC in 1974 with the addition of Wigan Corporation. Newhey, 14 March 2019.

D & G are based at Adderley Green, Stoke-on-Trent, and operate a variety of services in Cheshire and Staffordshire. No. 129 is a ubiquitous Optare Solo working to Altrincham, a town once in Cheshire but transferred to Greater Manchester in April 1974. The location is Wilmslow, now governed by Cheshire East Council following the abolition of Macclesfield Council and Cheshire County Council.

Glossop is situated in the High Peak district of Derbyshire close to the historic boundaries of Cheshire, Lancashire and Yorkshire. A stone-built Pennine town, Glossop is comparable socially and economically to the towns in nearby Tameside and Stockport. Greater Manchester PTE had a depot in Glossop for many years. Stotts of Oldham, Optare Solo MX07 NTG works into Glossop from Hyde during March 2019. The scenery around Glossop is a mixture of the bleak and spectacular, the Snake Pass being a notoriously difficult route to Sheffield during the winter.

Making steady progress along the often traffic clogged A6 at Hazel Grove is Stagecoach No. 12114. An Enviro400H, she carries Electric Hybrid branding for the busy service 192 between Manchester, Levenshulme, Stockport and Hazel Grove – a route that, according to Bus & Coach Week, carried 187,000 passengers per week before the pandemic.

Since privatisation, the Go-Ahead Group has expanded far and wide, with operations in Brighton, Oxford and elsewhere. Go North West acquired the Queens Road depot of First Manchester in June 2019 and now have a significant presence in Greater Manchester. Volvo B9TL/Wright Eclipse No. 37379 (3229) crosses Barton Bridge, over the Manchester Ship Canal, at Dumplington on 9 June 2019.

Arriva's Temsa Avenues are offbeat and rather ungainly buses. No. 4707 displays its angular lines at South Bank on a crisp 10 February 2020. Once dominated by heavy industry, South Bank has sadly suffered from the effects of deindustrialising – depopulation, urban decay and poverty. Cleveland Transit operated a depot for many years in South Bank, inherited from Teesside Municipal Transport (1968–74), which itself was formed from the Tees-side Railless Traction Board (1919–68).

Bowburn is one of many former mining villages that surround Durham. New housing estates have breathed fresh life into these communities, which are also increasingly popular with students at Durham University. Bowburn's most famous landmark, The Church of Christ the King, was demolished in 2007. Known as the 'Pineapple Church', it was post-war architecture at its most extreme. Arriva No. 1461 departs Bowburn for Bishop Auckland on 11 February 2020.

Keith's Coaches operate this impressive Irizar i6 complete with 9,186 cc engine, new in March 2015. The location is Hexham Road, Blucher village, on 3 March 2020, an area rich in Roman history. Hadrian's Wall, Milecastle 10 and the Vallum were all sited in the vicinity of Hexham Road. Nearby at Heddon-on-the-Wall, a substantial part of the wall is visible, which is thought to date from AD 122 or 123.

Wallsend is so called because it marks the end of Hadrian's Wall, which originally ran from Bowness-on-Solway (Mais/Maia) to Newcastle (Pons Aelius). The Roman fort protecting Wallsend was known as Segedunum and is located near the River Tyne. Famous for shipbuilding, Wallsend is a town in its own right and not just a suburb of Newcastle upon Tyne. At High Street West, Go North East Optare Solo No. 696 works towards Hadrian Park.

Heading back to the Arriva depot at Boathouse Lane, Stockton-on-Tees is No. 1427, a VDL SB200 with Wright Pulsar bodywork. Close by was the site of St John's Crossing, part of the Stockton & Darlington Railway of 1825. The ticket office survives as a hostel in an area that has seen considerable redevelopment since the 1980s.

Go North East No. 6052 carries the smart and distinctive Red Arrows branding. The Wright Eclipse Gemini 2 body married to a Volvo B9TL chassis has great visual presence as demonstrated here at Hetton-le-Hole. Several former Northern depots in the area have closed in the past few decades including High Spen, Murton, Philadelphia, Stanley and Winlaton.

Thornaby-on-Tees is a proudly independent town, located somewhat reluctantly in the borough of Stockton-on-Tees. Stagecoach Enviros Nos 26284 and 26282 have just past the railway station and town hall during the beginning of the pandemic in March 2021. This part of Thornaby was originally known as South Stockton and was historically part of the North Riding of Yorkshire.

On the fringe of Gateshead district is Eighton Banks, situated between Blackfell and Wrekenton. Go North East No. 3942, a Volvo B7TL/Wright Eclipse Gemini, was working towards Gateshead on 5 March 2020 with the *Angel of the North*, the often slow moving A1M and rationalised Tyne Marshalling Yard just out of sight.

Washington New Town is comprised of various settlements and industrial estates, often neatly landscaped and each distinctive in character. At Concord, Indigo-branded No. 680 was photographed operating service 84 to Washington Galleries, the town's large covered shopping mall, which is reminiscent of many in North America. Concord, 27 March 2020.

Part of the Optare Solos success has been its adaptability to different operating conditions; it is useful in both urban, suburban and rural environments. Hodgsons of Barnard Castle were using LJU 914 on the Newton Aycliffe town service in early 2020. Newton Aycliffe is another of the regions post-war towns, the others being Cramlington, Killingworth, Peterlee and Washington.

The village of Easington Lane lies at the southern tip of Tyne & Wear, one of many former mining villages within Sunderland district. At the Easington Lane Clock terminus, Go North East's Red Arrows-branded No. 6054 is about to leave for Newcastle, via Houghton-le-Spring and Washington, on 27 March 2020.

Swinging out of Consett bus station is Go North East No. 6917. After years of high unemployment following the closure of the BSC Consett works in 1980, the town has been going something of a renaissance. New houses, retail parks and unemployment close to the national average signify the new Consett. People associated with Consett include Denise Welch and Tony Mulholland.

Blaydon-on-Tyne bus station is situated close to the River Tyne and the busy Blaydon Highway. Most of the town centre is post-war in character and many of the suburbs climb the slopes towards Winlaton. Go North East No. 3995, a Scania N94UD/East Lancs OmniDekka combination, passes a Gateshead Central Taxis Fiat Ducato working to Clara Vale. The Scania was new to Go-North East's Brighton & Hove operation in Sussex.

A threatening sky dominates Stagecoach No. 27175 on the approach to the Tees (Newport) Bridge at Portrack. The Tees Bridge was opened in 1934 as a vertical-lift bridge and was a key crossing point for traffic, before the opening of the Tees Viaduct in 1975. The structure has been permanently locked down since 1990 as a result of a rapid post-war decline in shipping navigating the Portrack stretch of the River Tees. Taken on 1 July 2020.

The area comprising the former districts of Chester-le-Street and Derwentside are a mixture of semi-rural communities and small industrial towns. Close to Chester-le-Street and Gateshead is the village of Edmondsley, where Go North East Scania CN230UB/Scania Omnicity No. 5250 was working service 25 to Langley Park. Before deregulation, Northern General operated a red fleet within County Durham and a yellow fleet within Tyne & Wear causing identity problems for the unwary.

What a gas at Sunderland! Stagecoach No. 28010 is one of several Scania 'Gas Buses' operating in Wearside. Stagecoach services in the city can be traced back to Sunderland Corporation. The Corporation became part of Tyneside PTE in 1973, which was subsequently renamed as Tyne and Wear PTE in 1974. Busways, the successor of the PTE, was sold to its employees in 1989 and acquired by Stagecoach in July 1994. Pennywell, 10 March 2020.

The Scotswood area of Newcastle upon Tyne has witnessed considerable decline, demolition and depopulation since the Second World War. During March 2020, Stagecoach No. 19438 departs from Armstrong Road amidst bleak empty spaces ripe for redevelopment.

A heavy shower was lashing Stagecoach No. 39726 at Blakelaw in March 2020. Located on the western edge of Newcastle upon Tyne, Blakelaw has below average levels of car ownership, hence the importance of reliable public transport. Famous people to have lived in Newcastle upon Tyne have included Jean-Paul Marat, the subject of David's painting *The Death of Marat* in 1793, and philosopher Ludwig Wittgenstein. Wittgenstein was famous for his impenetrable but influential *Tractatus Logico-Philsophicus* of 1921.

Possibly one of Go North East's less attractive liveries is the Red Kite brand. Eye-catching certainly, but No. 6121 looks messy and slightly sinister on this Wright-bodied VolvoB9TL at Sunniside, Tyne & Wear. Photographed on 20 March 2020.

Brightening up a cold and cloudy 20 March 2020 is Go North East No. 5406. Resplendent in two-tone green Coast & Country branding, she is a Wright Streetlite DF Max Micro-Hybrid – yet another intricate name for a bus. The location is Pelton, County Durham.

Berwick-upon-Tweed was extremely busy on 21 March 2020 as shoppers from a wide area stocked up on supplies before the COVID-19 lockdown. Woody's Taxis and Executive Travel were operating this Volkswagen Transporter/Bluebird Tucana combination first registered in February 2010. Berwick-upon-Tweed has switched between Scotland and England numerous times and gives its name to an abolished Scottish county called Berwickshire. For the present time, it constitutes a part of Northumberland and remains England's most northerly town.

In a rural county like Northumberland, a coaching and farming town like Belford qualifies as an urban environment! Less busy that it was in the days of the stagecoach, Belford has a sleepy atmosphere due to the A1 bypass. Bereft of customers, Travelsure's Optare Solo YNO6 LCM was photographed before departure to Alnwick. Belford on 21 March 2020.

The sleek, handsome lines of the bestselling Mercedes-Benz Citaro can be seen in this view of Go North East No. 5359. Carrying Connections 4 branding, she was photographed at North View Terrace, Colliery Row, on 23 March 2020.

Go North East is an enthusiastic user of the Optare Solo. The driver of No. 722 answers the queries of some potential passengers at Heworth Metro, Felling, during March 2020. The name Felling is thought to be derived from the clearing of wood and forest on the north bank of the Tyne.

Ageing Alexander Dennis Dart No. 35188 still looks in excellent condition when photographed at Stanhope Road in the West Park area of South Shields. A town of considerable antiquity, South Shields is an unusual mixture of coastal resort, industrial centre and shopping town. Roads around South Shields Roman fort are appropriately named Trajan, Vespasian and Julian. South Shields Corporation joined Newcastle Transport as part of the new Tyneside PTE in 1970, although both had separate operating areas.

The pandemic caused serious disruption and alterations to bus services throughout England in March 2020. Reflecting decreased patronage, Go North East used many non-standard buses on the X10 express between Tyneside and Teesside. In Green Arrow branding for the Gateshead area, No. 5492 makes an unusual appearance on the X10 roster at West Road, Billingham.

Contiguous with Stockton-on-Tees is the village of Norton, once more important than the former. Norton has a distinct character with a wide green, duck pond and architecturally cohesive High Street. Turning towards Stockton-on-Tees from the Norton Grange estate, previously known as Blue Hall, Stagecoach No. 26282 was pictured working route 38 to Middlesbrough.

Illustrating Go North East's commitment to high-quality transport, X-lines-branded No. 6304 works through heavy rain during July 2020. Photographed at Tindale Crescent, this unmistakable bus features Wi-Fi and 'Talking Bus' facilities – a far cry from the days OK Motor Services and United. Service X21 connects Bishop Auckland with Newcastle upon Tyne via Durham.

Liverton Mines is on the fringe of Teesside's built-up area, very much a semi-rural area close to the North York Moors National Park. Arriva No. 1451 was snapped on the final leg of its journey from Middlesbrough to Easington (Redcar & Cleveland) on a humid afternoon on 7 July 2020. The nearby Loftus depot was closed in 2009 with the loss of twenty jobs.

Working out of Newcastle-upon-Tyne's west end is Stagecoach No. 11292 at Stanhope Street, Arthur's Hill. The suburb stands on a promience between Elswick and Fenham. Great swathes of Arthur's Hill have been reconstructed and today the population is extremely diverse. Africans, Arabs, Eastern Europeans, and South Asians all form a large proportion of the population.

Chopwell is a high altitude settlement in the former Tyne & Wear Metropolitan County. No. 6073, a sturdy Volvo B9TL/Wright Gemini 2, was photographed on the last part of the journey to Blackhall Mill. For a time Chopwell was nicknamed 'Little Moscow' due to local support for the Communist party.

At Billingham, Stagecoach No. 27245 traverses Central Avenue close to the location of the now demolished Billingham House, a grand office block built by ICI and more in keeping with the business districts of Birmingham, Bristol, and London. Beneath the largely modern face of Billingham lies an older Anglo-Saxon settlement. St Cuthbert's Church has an Anglo-Saxon tower and during the Black Death of 1348/9, about a third of the population died from the plague.

Seaton Carew railway station is situated to the left of this photograph. Opened in 1841 as Seaton by the Stockton & Hartlepool Railway, the site was renamed Seaton Carew in 1872. The NER buildings were demolished in the 1970s and today the facilities are basic but adequate. Passing under the railway line is Stagecoach No. 39661, photographed on 8 June 2020.

Haltwhistle is claimed by some to be the centre of Great Britain – at least while the Union lasts! Contributing their share to service 685 between Carlisle and Newcastle, Arriva were using this grimly painted VDL SB200/Wright combination during the pandemic summer of 2020.

Go North East now operate from the former Arriva and United Automobile Services depot at Hexham. It is rather strange to see Go North East, familiar to many as Northern, operating in rural Northumberland. Services from Hexham reach Tyneside, Allendale, Bellingham, Haltwhistle and even Alston. A Tynedale-branded Optare Solo poses with stable mates at Hexham depot in the summer of 2020.

Rothbury is an inland resort set against the beautiful Simonside Hills and is about as urban as you can get in this part of Northumberland. Arriving at the bus stance No. 7515, a Dennis Trident 2/Alexander Enviro400, was heading towards Morpeth before terminating at Newcastle upon Tyne. Before local government reorganisation, Rothbury was located in the Alnwick district of Northumberland.

The MAN 18.220 with Alexander or ADL ALX300 bodywork once played a significant role in the Stagecoach fleet. New in 2004, No. 22062 was one of a dwindling number still left in service when photographed at Portrack Lane, Stockton-on-Tees. The type operated from numerous Stagecoach depots including Ashton-under-Lyne, Cambridge, Dundee, Oxford, Stockport, and in this case Stockton-on-Tees.

The harsh modern architecture surrounding Pontefract bus station gives little clue to the long and interesting history of the town. Arriva No. 171, a Wright-bodied Volvo B5LH, carries distinctive Hybrid Technology branding. Richard II was probably murdered at Pontefract Castle in 1400. The infamous Richard III had Sir Richard Grey and Anthony Woodville executed at the castle in 1483. The castle was largely dismantled from 1649 and little remains today. March 2021.

Heritage liveries have proved popular in recent years. Stagecoach No. 10030 carries Ribble's short-lived but attractive post-deregulation livery. At deregulation, Ribble lost her Merseyside services to a resurrected North Western, and her Cumbrian services to an expanded Cumberland. These losses were offset by expansion in Greater Manchester and elsewhere. Service 100 links Lancaster University with Morecambe via Hala, Torrisholme and Bare. Taken on 2 November 2020 at South Road, Lancaster.

In mid-July 2021 England experienced a tiring and interminable heatwave. In Quernmore, Lancashire, part of the road melted resulting in dangerous conditions for motorists. At Longridge in the Ribble Valley district, Pilkington's Optare Solo KX15 BMY was pictured at Berry Lane as the temperature began its inexorable rise on 17 July 2021.

In sweltering heat, a bus enthusiast has made a dash to photograph Stagecoach No. 15566, resplendent in Ribble Timesaver heritage branding. The location is Tithebarn Street, Preston, an area of the city subjected to considerable post-war redevelopment. Famous people associated with Preston include Sir Richard Arkwright, John Inman and Ranvir Singh.

Preston bus station opened in 1969 and represents the era's architecture at its boldest. Now listed, the bus station has been renovated and the side previously used by Preston Bus pedestrianised. Oversized for today's transport needs, the combined bus station and multistorey car park stands up better than many other similar bus stations of the era. Nominees for the worst bus stations ever: Aylesbury, Canterbury, Chatham Pentagon, Hanley, Ilfracombe, Lincoln, Northampton, Slough, Whitley Bay?

One of Preston Bus' more elderly buses is No. 40632, a Dennis Trident/Plaxton President combination new in 2003 with 8,268 cc engine. Preston Bus is now owned by Rotola, following a brief but controversial period of Stagecoach ownership.

Preston Bus No. 20771 leaves the bus station in sweltering heat on 17 July 2020 for Holme Slack. Every twenty years Preston holds a Guild Merchant, an honour conferred on the town in 1179 by Henry II. The last Preston Guild was held in 2012.

The old Nelson bus station, an unedifying testament to the decline in architectural standards during the late twentieth century, has been demolished and replaced by a new interchange closer to the railway station. An unidentified Transdev Ribble Country-branded Mercedes-Benz awaits custom at Nelson Interchange on 24 July 2021. Beautiful countryside surrounds Nelson with Boulsworth Hill and Pendle Hill being notable summits.

Transdev operate several transport fleets in the north of England including The Blackburn Bus Company, The Burnley Bus Company, Coastliner and Rosso. Notable brandings include Cityzap, Dalesway, Mainline and Witchway – the latter a reference to the Pendle witches. Demonstrating Mainline branding is Optare Versa No. 255, photographed at Primet Bridge, Colne, during July 2021.

Between Blackburn and Burnley is the Borough of Hyndburn. Accrington is the dominant town, with Church, Clayton-le-Moors, Great Harwood and Oswaldtwistle striving for their individual identity within the borough. East Lancashire's typically hilly countryside forms a backdrop for Blackburn Bus Co. No. 100 at Rishton. She was working the trunk route 152 between Burnley and Preston. Resplendent in Ribble anniversary livery, she is an ageing but still stylish Volvo B7TL/Wright Eclipse Gemini combination, originally registered YJ04 LYG.

The Blackburn Bus Company's No. 221 has just passed under the Church & Oswaldtwistle railway station bridge. Mining and mills formed the backbone of Oswaldtwistle's industrial history. Today Oswaldtwistle Mills are a tourist attraction but like considerable swathes of East Lancashire unemployment remains stubbornly high. Taken at Church, Lancashire, July 2021.

Fleetwood along with Blackpool, Nelson and St Annes is a nineteenth-century creation. Peter Hesketh-Fleetwood planned Fleetwood as railway cum port town on the River Wyre. After a brief boom, Hesketh-Fleetwood's dream failed and he died in poverty. Today Fleetwood is a holiday and shopping town. At Affinity Outlet Lancashire, Blackpool Transport No. 422, an ADL E400 City 422, was pictured on layover before working service 1 to Starr Gate. Taken on 25 July 2021.

Any visit to the Fylde coast necessitates a ride on a tram. Trundling along Lord Street, Fleetwood, was this stylish heritage tram known as a 'Boat'. She was built in 1934 by English Electric at Preston. Fleetwood is the chief town in the Lancashire district of Wyre, a district which includes a considerable amount of rural terrain around Garstang.

Despite a modern appearance Blackpool Tram No. 707 was actually constructed in 1934, part of a batch known as Balloons. Some of the fleet were rebuilt at the turn of this century and became known as 'Millenniums'. Looking rather angular after modification in 1998, English Electric No. 707 is seen against Bispham's period tram station wearing the old Blackpool green and cream livery. Photograph taken on 25 July 2021 from Red Bank, Bispham.

Cleveleys is a lively but less brash resort than Blackpool. Often paired with its neighbour Thornton, as Thornton-Cleveleys, the town has excellent views of the Irish Sea and a more suburban ambience than Blackpool. At the town's small bus station, Coastliner Buses Optare Solo PX04 DLV prepares to depart for Poulton-le-Fylde. She was new to Stagecoach Ribble in 2004.

A rather messy scene at Nelson showing the site of the former bus station at Broadway and Holme Street. Transdev 265 and 256 are working out to Burnley and Trawden respectively. Nelson was named after the Nelson Inn public house and was a new textile town based on the pre-existing settlements of Little and Great Marsden.

Skelmersdale, West Lancashire, was designated as a New Town in 1961. The town neatly separates housing estates, industry and arterial roads in typical New Town style. The covered Concourse Shopping Centre near the River Tawd is Skelmerdale's epicentre. Arriva No. 3021 had just alighted passengers at the elevated bus station on 31 July 2020.

Speke is situated on the edge of the city of Liverpool and famous for the wonderful Speke Hall and a notoriously inefficient, strike prone and now closed Triumph factory. Speke was also briefly the residence of Paul McCartney and George Harrison. Photographed at Western Avenue on 31 July 2021 is Arriva No. 4811, a hybrid Volvo B5LH Wright Gemini 3. Liverpool John Lennon Airport is out of shot.

The port of Garston abuts the River Mersey and the first dock was opened in 1793. A part of Liverpool since 1902, Garston is now an important container and shipping port located several miles downstream from the better-known docks at Bootle and Seaforth. Liverpool had just been stripped of World Heritage Status when Stagecoach No. 10833 was photographed at Garston on 31 July 2021.

Widnes once had the dubious title of being Britain's most polluted town. Rival claimants could have included Manchester and Haverton Hill. Widnes railway station was also the inspiration of Simon and Garfunkel's 'Homeward Bound'. At Widnes, Arriva No. 5016, a MAN EcoCity (Gas Bus)/Caetano combination, enters Vicarage Road. Sadly, Halton Transport the successor of Widnes Corporation ceased trading in January 2020.

Entering Penketh at Widnes Road in the borough of Warrington is a second photograph of Arriva No. 5010. Warrington has suffered something of an identity crisis since 1974. Historically a Lancashire town, Warrington was placed into Cheshire in 1974. Now a unitary authority, Warrington includes land in what is historically Cheshire and Lancashire. People associated with Warrington include Chris Evans, Burt Kwouk and Marta Zielinska.

Rainhill is situated within the St Helens district of Merseyside. Pictured outside Loyola Hall, we see Cumfybus Optare Solo YJ12 GXB. She was photographed at Warrington Road, Rainhill Stoops on the circular service 289 to St Helens via Prescot. Cumfybus are based at Southport, an elegant seaside resort on the northerly tip of the old Merseyside Metropolitan County.

St Helens developed as the epicentre of Britain's glass industry. Firms such as the British Cast Plate Company and Pilkington's were internationally renowned. Arriva No. 2615, a VDL SB120/Plaxton Centro combination, was snapped at Bridge Street, St Helens, bound for Sutton Heath. St Helens Corporation was subsumed by Merseyside PTE in 1974.

Working through Haydock, best known for its racecourse, is Arriva VDL DB300/Wright Eclipse Gemini 2 No. 4435. Haydock was once an important coal mining centre. The last mine known as Wood Pit closed in 1971. St Edward Arrowsmith, the Catholic martyr, was born in Haydock in 1585 and executed in 1628. Parts of St Edward's relics are housed in nearby Ashton-in-Makerfield.

A rear view shot of Stagecoach No. 19191 and a frontal picture of No. 18441 at Ashton-in-Makerfield. There are three settlements in Greater Manchester named Ashton, the other two being Ashton-under-Lyne and Ashton-upon-Mersey. Makerfield is a name given to the area of Lancashire roughly bounded by St Helens and Wigan, and including Ince-in-Makerfield. Newton-in-Makerfield was renamed as Newton-le-Willows.

Diamond No. 40829, a Wright StreetDeck, represents Rotala's huge investment in new stock during 2020. Rotala was formed in 2005 and purchased First's Bolton services in August 2019. The location is Kearsley, Greater Manchester, on 1 August 2021. The left side of the road is considered to be Farnworth, in contrast to Kearsley on the right! Both districts were absorbed by Bolton in 1974.

The stylised 'M' is a sign one is within Greater Manchester. The *Manchester Evening News* reported in 2011 that the original logo was the third most recognised transport brand in the UK. Photographed on layover at Farnworth bus station is Metro Shuttle-branded YJ11 ENU, an Optare Versa in service with Vision Bus of Blackrod. The service is funded by Transport for Greater Manchester and Bolton Council. Farnworth, 1 August 2020.

On 1 August 2020 Diamond No. 40840 prepares to leave Loxham Street, Moses Gate, for Bury. The area has a series of religious connotations – the location is Moses Gate (meaning 'the way across the mosses') and St Peters Way flyover, numbered the A666, is carrying traffic to Bolton. The large Sughra Mosque, a local landmark, is close by at Granville Street.

The decommissioned Fiddler's Ferry Power Station at Cuerdley Cross forms the backdrop for No. 101 in the Warrington's Own Buses fleet. She is an Optare Versa, resplendent in Blue Line branding and was photographed approaching Penketh. Opened in 1971, the power station is a major landmark in the area and can be seen as far away as Flintshire and Saddleworth. Warrington, August 2021.

Until 1969 when it was absorbed by SELNEC, the small Lancashire town of Ramsbottom operated a small bus fleet. Representing contemporary bus services in Ramsbottom is Transdev No. 1864 pictured about to turn onto Manchester Road. Ramsbottom lost her independence in 1974, becoming part of an enlarged Bury. Neighbouring Bacup, Haslingden and Rawtenstall remained in Lancashire.

Transdev No. 230 carries the Blackburn Bus Company identity on of one of the numerous Optare Versas to operate around East Lancashire. Having just cleared the railway line at Whalley Road, Accrington, she will call into the George Slynn bus station, which opened in 2016 at a cost of £6.4 million. The bus station was named in honour of Hyndburn councillor and transport advocate George Slynn, who died in 2009.

Higher Walton is situated in the South Ribble district of Lancashire, located between Preston and Chorley. Working the busy 152 for Transdev's Blackburn Bus Company is No. 2763. Carrying Pride of the North branding, she is seen passing the Mill Tavern close to the River Darwen. Previous Transdev brandings in Lancashire included The Whalley Ranger (Blackburn) and Lancashire United.

Cumbria Classic Coaches, based at Ravenstonedale, are best known for running heritage bus services. A more conventional bus is this DAF DB250/East Lancs combination photographed at Station Road, Kendal. She was previously in service with Blackpool Transport as No. 364. Kendal, located beside the River Kent, means 'Kent-dale', the full title of the town being Kirkby Kendal.

Cockermouth was the birthplace of Fletcher Christian, immortalised by Clark Gable in the 1935 adaptation of *Mutiny on the Bounty*. The town's other famous son is the romantic poet William Wordsworth, who's inspired, often mystical verse captured the spirit of the Lakeland landscape. Pictured at the Earl of Mayo statue is Stagecoach Mercedes-Benz Sprinter City No. 44009.

Seaton Carew's art deco-style bus station was in danger of demolition at one time. On a cold 27 August 2021, Go North East trainers Nos 4965 and 5202 were awaiting the next stage of their educational duties around Hartlepool. Branded as Join the Team, these Scania L94UBs carry Wright Solar bodywork and promotional advertising about the benefits of working for Go North East. As might be expected, bus companies have high levels of staff turnover.

Arriva's X21 service connects Newcastle upon Tyne with Newbiggin-by-the-Sea. The latter town is associated with coal mining and fishing, and thanks to the endeavours of Newbiggin Town Council is now undergoing something of a renaissance. Arriva No. 7750 carries Sapphire branding and was seen at the Creswell Arms, Newbiggin-by-the-Sea.

The busy A677 at Copy Nook, Audley, is the location for a pair of Optare Versas operated by the Blackburn Bus Company. Leading is No. 232 and following behind is sister No. 231. Blackburn Transport is yet another defunct municipal operator, having sold out to Transdev Blazefield on 22 January 2007. Blackburn had absorbed Darwen Corporation in 1974 and had used various shades of green for fleet livery over the years. Transdev retain the Blackburn depot at Intack. Audley, 4 September 2021.

Photographed at Dunoon Drive, Shadsworth, is ageing No. 1100 of the Blackburn Bus Company. A Volvo B10BLE/Wright Renown combination, she is beginning her return journey to Clitheroe via Blackburn town centre on 4 September 2021.

On 4 September 2021, B & N Coaches Yutong collects a lively group at Haslingden, Lancashire. A coach with some presence, even in plain white, she was new in November 2018. For many years Haslingden was the home of Irish Nationalist Michael Davitt, who died in 1906.

The Optare Solo is well suited for the hilly and narrow roads around east Lancaster. Stagecoach No. 47963 descends Kirkes Road, Moorlands, on service 15. The Moorlands and Freehold areas of the city have impressive views of Morecambe Bay and Cumbria. Close by is the busy M6 and the beautiful moors of the Forest of Bowland.

Looking like a box on wheels is this Little Hotline-branded Mercedes-Benz Sprinter/Mellor Strata Ultra combination at Walton-le-Dale, a settlement in South Ribble. Walton Bridge was the scene of Civil War skirmishes in 1644. The First Battle of Preston in 1648 was fought around Walton-le-Dale and was effectively the death knell for the King Charles I and the Royalist cause. Taken on 4 September 2021.

Egremont is a remote, former industrial town close to the relatively unknown Cumbrian coast. Historically a Cumberland town, Egremont was placed into the new Copeland district of Cumbria in April 1974. With local government reorganisation due, Egremont will form part of the new Cumberland Council from April 2023. In the town centre, Stagecoach No. 15686 prepares for a journey north to Maryport.

Preston Bus housed their diverse fleet at the old Corporation depot at Deepdale Road. Photographed in the deport yard is Wright StreetLite No. 20185, previously with sister company Diamond Bus. Local legend says that if you listen carefully, you can still hear the melodic sounds of the long-departed Leyland Panthers and Atlanteans in the now closed depot.

Perhaps not quite an urban environment, but nevertheless worthy of inclusion, is this study of Stagecoach No. 11207. The location is the massive University of Lancaster site at Bailrigg. The university opened in 1964 and has grown extensively in the intervening years. The campus was surprisingly quiet on 4 September 2021 as the new semester had not started. The bus is of course a trusty integral Alexander Dennis Enviro400.

Photographed crossing the High Level Bridge, Stagecoach Optare Solo No. 47143 works into Barrow Island bound for Biggar Bank on Walney Island. The Michaelson Road Bridge was opened in 1964, replacing a structure from 1884. Below are Devonshire and Buccleuch Docks and in the distance the tower of Barrow Town Hall. Taken on 5 September 2021.

The capital of Calderdale Metropolitan Borough is Halifax. The town rests in a spectacular setting, surrounded by steep hills and what is left of the textile mills. Leaving Halifax on the busy A58 at New Bank is First No. 69687, seen here in the company of a Scania lorry. The bus will continue up the A58 and through a dramatic deep cutting towards Stump Cross, Halifax. Taken on September 2021.

In pouring rain, Arriva's Enviro400 No. 1929 makes slow progress through Huddersfield Road, Scout Hill. She is just about to pass under the former Spen Valley line into Ravensthorpe. Nearby was the site of the long-demolished Thornhill Power Station and Lees Hall. Dewsbury, 9 September 2021.

In absolutely atrocious weather conditions, Arriva No. 1975, an Alexander Dennis Enviro400, stands unperturbed outside Heckmondwike depot on 9 September 2021. Drivers were staying in the depot safe from spectacular lightning bolts and rain of almost biblical intensity. Heckmondwike is situated in the heavy woollen district of Kirklees. The town has a notably ostentatious Independent Chapel (Congregational), which was constructed in 1890.

Attercliffe is situated in Sheffield's industrial Don Valley, to the east of the city centre. Sports facilities, retail parks and hotels have helped fill the gap left by the closure of numerous industrial plants. Photographed at Attercliffe Common is First South Yorkshire No. 37498, a Volvo B9TL with Wright bodywork captured working the X1 to Maltby on 9 September 2021.

Brightside Lane, Sheffield, is more in keeping with the Don Valley's image as a centre of heavy industry. Amidst steelworks including the renowned Sheffield Forgemasters, First No. 37112 heads north-east to the railway town of Doncaster on 10 September 2021.

An early morning shot of First No. 69512 at Masbrough. In the distance is Rotherham town centre, which includes Bridge Chapel, erected in 1483 and restored in 1924. Rotherham became one of the four constituent boroughs of South Yorkshire in 1974. Besides Rotherham, the district also includes Dinnington, Maltby, Swinton, Wath-upon-Dearne and numerous villages such as Treeton, Wales and Wentworth.

Contrasting Stagecoach liveries outside Rawmarsh depot to the north of Rotherham. On the left, No. 26031 carries the bright and cheerful new corporate colours. On the right, No. 22556 is attired in the previous and somewhat undistinguished livery. Rawmarsh depot was of course Yorkshire Traction property before the Stagecoach takeover in 2005. 10 September 2021.

Entering Mexborough is this smart little Enviro200 operated by Powells of Hellaby. She is working the X20 between Doncaster and Barnsley. Mexborough is an industrial town noted in the past for ceramics, coal mining, quarrying and brick making. Located within the Doncaster district of South Yorkshire, the town was hard hit by deindustrialisation from the 1980s.

Enviro300 No. 37145 carries the dynamic new corporate Stagecoach livery at Doncaster Road, Barnsley. Barnsley is now a metropolitan borough having subsumed various outlying settlements including Grimethorpe, Hoyland, Penistone, Thurnscoe, Wombwell and a portion of the Peak District National Park. In South Yorkshire PTE days, Yorkshire Traction was the dominant operator in Barnsley district.

Barnsley bus station has long been an exceptionally busy terminus due in part to below average levels of car ownership. On 10 September 2021, various buses are visible in the clean and modern surroundings of the Interchange. Gone is the acrid smoke and windswept stands of the old Yorkshire Traction terminal, although the reversing horns remain as loud as ever.

Barnsley bus station is now known as Barnsley Interchange. On the right, train No. 158908 collects passengers at the railway station side of the Interchange. To the left, Stagecoach buses Nos 36988 and 22952 are pictured in the bus station. The acclaimed Ken Loach film *Kes* was made around the Barnsley area in 1969. Locations included Lundwood, St Helens, Tankersley and the town of Hoyland.

Stagecoach Gold branding is carried by No. 1120, at Barnsley. She is working the flagship X17 to Sheffield and Chesterfield. Barnsley has seen considerable post-war redevelopment, both in the 1960s and at the current time. Only a few streets in the town give a sense of what Barnsley would have been like before the advent of industry. The Domesday Book of 1086 records Barnsley as 'Berneslai'.

Close to the West Yorkshire boundary is the village of Darton, although it is virtually contiguous with Barnsley town, forming a chain of settlements with Mapplewell, Stain Cross, Athersley and Smithies. Stagecoach No. 22615, a MAN 18.240/Alexander Dennis Enviro300, collects a sole passenger for service 93 to Woolley Grange on 10 September 2021.

TLC Travel Ltd are based in Bradford. The fleet includes this neat little Dennis Dart/Alexander Enviro200. Working service 660 to Shipley Glen, No. 13981 climbs up Rockwell Lane at Thorpe Edge. In the far distance Rawdon and Horsforth sit on top of the green hills above the River Aire. Bradford, 10 September 2021.

Tyersal is in the Bradford BD4 postcode but is split between the cities of Bradford and Leeds. On the Pudsey side of Tyersal, within Leeds district, First No. 69576 works service 630 to Bradford, a distance of about 2 miles.

Leeds Road, Bradley, is the location of First No. 30949, a Volvo B7TL/Alexander ALX400 combination, still giving good service in September 2021. Bradley is situated east of Huddersfield, close to the site of Kirklees Priory and the alleged grave of Robin Hood, just east of Wakefield Road.

The charming Little Harwood war memorial contrasts with the surrounding clutter – signs, traffic lights and lamp standards. The clock tower was unveiled in 1923 as a memorial to those who fell in the First World War. Blackburn Private Hire was using this all-white Optare Solo, YJ62 FHU, on the weekly service between Blackburn and Sunnybower. Photographed at Whalley Old Road, Little Harwood on 15 September 2021.

High rise flats constructed in the early 1960s dominate the area around Birley Street, Daisyfield. On 15 September 2021, Blackburn Private Hire's Optare Solo YJ62 FHU prepares to loop around the tower blocks on service 3 to nearby Blackburn town centre. Obscured by the tower block is St Alban's Roman Catholic Church, constructed in stages around 1824–26, 1861 and 1900–01. St Alban's is a key focal point for Blackburn's once substantial Catholic population.

Dalton-in-Furness was a Lancashire town until it was reluctantly moved into Cumbria in 1974. Situated between Barrow-in-Furness and Ulverston, Dalton was once the administrative centre of the Furness Peninsula and later an important industrial town, specialising in iron ore mining and stone quarries. The Furness Brick & Tile Co. Ltd is still operating today at Askham-in-Furness. Working out to Kendal, Stagecoach No. 15698, a Scania N230/Alexander Dennis Enviro400, was photographed ascending Broughton Road during September 2021.

A view from the east side of Preston close to the River Ribble and Britain's first motorway, the M6. Longridge Coaches were using this ageing Dennis Trident/ Alexander ALX400 combination. New to Stagecoach Manchester in January 2006, she was photographed at Tudor Avenue, Farringdon Park, on 23 September 2021.

Photographed at Blackburn Road, Great Harwood, is No. 229, an Optare Versa in the Blackburn Bus Company fleet. In 1974, Great Harwood together with Clayton-le-Moors and Rishton were placed in the then new borough of Hyndburn. To avoid giving prominence to Accrington, the name Hyndburn was chosen, this being a river which flows through the district known as the Hyndburn Brook.

The terraced houses and small shopping street of Kings Road, North Ormesby, form the backdrop for Arriva No. 1552. Working service 5A to Guisbrorough, she is a Sapphire-branded Wright Streetlite. Out of view is the marketplace, although the tower of Holy Trinity Church is just visible – the chancel and nave were destroyed by a conflagration in 1977.

With the destination already set for the return journey to Darlington's Branksome Estate, Arriva No. 4813 traverses Coombe Drive, Red Hall, on 28 September 2021. The now forgotten Children's Film Foundation picture *Anoop and the Elephant* was shot around Darlington in the 1970s.

Barnoldswick is a West Riding town which, to the chagrin of its residents, was placed into the Pendle district of Lancashire in 1974. The town is pronounced 'Baa-lik'. Pilkington Bus of Accrington was operating the town service on 1 October 2021 with smart Optare Solo YJ60 KFP.

With the dramatic heights of Pendle Hill in the background, Mainline No. 271 was running late as it approached the terminus at Lane House Lane, Trawden. Standing 1,827 feet above sea level, Pendle Hill was the spot where George Fox, the founder of the Quakers, had his life-changing religious vision in 1652. Trawden, 1 October 2021.

Photographed at Victoria Road, Earby, is Gold-branded Stagecoach No. 27272, working service 280 from Skipton to Preston. Earby is another prim industrial town transferred from Yorkshire to Lancashire in 1974. The town's railway station closed in 1970, severing what could now be a useful commuter link into East Lancashire. Earby, October 2021.

Transdev No. 569 is a Volvo B10BLE/Wright Renown new to the Keighley & District operation, just over the moors, in December 2000. Despite the dull, rather anonymous white livery, she looks in fine condition, although the destination should read 'Burnley' rather than Higherford. The location is Gisburn Road, Barrowford, in October 2021.

The Stagecoach depot serving Lancaster district is situated at Whitegate on Morecambe's White Lund Industrial Estate. Stagecoach are the successor to Ribble and the former municipal operators based around the River Lune. Stagecoach No. 22610, a MAN 18.240 with ADL Enviro300 bodywork, leaves the depot on a dismal autumn day in October 2021. Morecambe and Heysham Corporation merged with Lancaster in 1974, forming an enlarged Lancaster City Transport. The undertaking was dissolved in August 1993 following intense competition from Stagecoach.

Torrisholme is one of the villages that formed what became the seaside resort of Morecambe, the other villages being Bare and Poulton-le-Sands. The nucleus of these settlements is apparent too if one wanders the streets of Morecambe. At Torrisholme Square, Stagecoach No. 11206, an integral Alexander Dennis Enviro400, is seen against a cluttered and gloomy backdrop in October 2021.

Many Lancashire towns east of the M6 have a hilly topography with Blackburn being no exception. Ascending North Road, Queen's Park, is Moving People's Y176 CFS, a Dennis Dart SLF/Plaxton Pointer new to Lothian. Out of shot to the left stood the ill-fated Queen's Park flats, an unsuccessful high rise housing scheme demolished in 2002. Blackpool had a similar estate with the same name, which was demolished in 2016. In the distance are Audley Range, Greenbank and Little Harwood. Queen's Park, 29 October 2021.

Fishwick is a cosmopolitan district of Preston. There is a significant Asian Eastern European population, adding diversity to an area close to the pretty banks of the River Ribble. Preston Bus No. 30117 is a Scania Omnilink K230UB traversing a rain-soaked New Hall Lane, Fishwick, on 29 October 2021.

Over at Deepdale, Preston Bus Scania Omnidekka/East Lancashire No. 40406 shares depot space with on loan Diamond-branded No. 40759 and an unidentified Optare Solo.

The Royal Preston Hospital is a major NHS facility in the Sharoe Green area of Fulwood. Until 1974, Fulwood was an independent urban district to the north of Preston, noted for its affluence and desirable properties. Preston Bus No. 40808, a Wright StreetDeck, was photographed on layover at the hospital bus stance on 29 October 2021.

The Frenchwood area of Preston was for years the headquarters of Ribble Motor Services, though the company was initially based in the village of Gregson Lane in South Ribble. Large parts of the Ribble site have been cleared; nevertheless the depot plays an important role in the current Stagecoach infrastructure. In Royal British Legion livery, No. 10534, an Alexander Dennis Enviro400, poses gracefully at the Selborne Street exit of Frenchwood depot, Preston, on 29 October 2021.

Parked cars and limited road space can be a problem for large buses at Wensley Road, Wensley Fold. Blackburn Private Hire's Optare Versa has few problems as it works service 10 to Lammack. Wensley Fold, 29 October 2021.

Stagecoach No. 15567 has just entered the borough of Blackburn with Darwen at Beardwood. In the background is the rural parish of Mellor in the Ribble Valley. Preston New Road, Blackburn, is the precise location of this typical Stagecoach Scania N230UD/Enviro400 combination.

One of the older double-deckers in the Stagecoach Cumbria & North Lancashire fleet is No. 18364. New in October 2005, she is an Alexander Dennis Trident/Alexander ALX400 combination pictured at Haws Hill, Carnforth.

The minarets of the Masjide Noorul Islam (Mosque) rise like candle sticks above terraced housing at Audley Range, Blackburn. Moving People operate this Optare Solo, YJO4 CCW, named *Jessica*. She was photographed on service 33 between Darwen and Blackburn.

The Leeds Guided Busway was opened along the A61 to much fanfare in 1995 but recent reports suggest that Leeds will abandon the A61 guided busway in the near future. One of the services not using the corridor is First No. 35284, a Wright StreetDeck pictured at King Lane, Moortown. Taken on 4 November 2021.

The A61 guided busway avoids Harrogate Road, Chapel Allerton, taking the faster Scott Hall Road to Leeds. Working the flagship service 36 between Harrogate and Leeds at Harrogate Road is Transdev No. 3625. A Volvo B5TL/Wright Eclipse Gemini 3, she is luxuriously equipped for a public service vehicle. Service 36 once reached Ripon, in the hands of utilitarian Bristol VRs and Leyland Nationals operated by West Yorkshire and United. Chapel Allerton, 4 November 2021.

Harehills is a densely populated and racially diverse part of east Leeds. Bringing back memories of the past is First No. 37675, masquerading as West Yorkshire Road Car No. 1812. During PTE days, many West Yorkshire buses were painted in Verona green. The last official West Yorkshire Road Car service was operated from Bradford in 1989.

First operate a number of school bus routes on behalf of West Yorkshire Metro, once known as West Yorkshire PTE. In My Bus branding, BMC Condor No. 68696 has just collected a group of students for a day of teaching and learning at Birkby Hall Road, Huddersfield. BMC is a Turkish automotive company founded in 1964 in partnership with the British Motor Corporation, which held a 26 per cent share. Birkby, 5 November 2021.

Golcar is high up above Huddersfield, one of numerous settlements that merge into each other to form the West Yorkshire conurbation. Looking bright and welcoming in Team Pennine branding, Transdev's ADL E20D/Enviro200 is pictured on 5 November 2021. She was one of numerous buses around the country adorned with a poppy in anticipation of Remembrance Day. The location is Swallow Lane, Golcar.

The much-missed J. J. Longstaff & Sons operated a small coach fleet from their base in Mirfield. A bus service was also operated between Mirfield and Dewsbury using everything from a Northern Counties-bodied Leyland Atlantean to a 1996 Dennis Lance. Longstaff ceased trading in 2011, but the name is still used by A. Lyles & Son of Batley. Resplendent in Longstaff livery, Optare Metrocity YJ16 DFF stands against bright sunshine at Huddersfield Road, Mirfield, during November 2021.

High rise flats at Little London provide a rather stark backdrop to First No. 37723 at Roundhay Road, Chapeltown. Several tower blocks in Leeds and other cities including Dundee and Glasgow have been levelled in recent years – yet high rise private apartments continue to sprout up all over the country! Since 1967, Chapeltown has hosted the annual Leeds West Indian Carnival, a colourful and vibrant occasion suspended during the pandemic. Leeds, 5 November 2021.

Halifax and more surprisingly Sowerby Bridge have tall tower blocks set against the steep Pennine hills. In Halifax, First No. 37063, a Volvo B9TL/Wright Eclipse Gemini, works into the town centre after a run to Calder High School, Mytholmroyd. In the distance the A58 Burdock Way flyover and tower blocks at Boothtown add a sense of modernity to a strangely old-fashioned town.

For years Bingley suffered terrible traffic congestion as traffic flowed between Skipton, Keighley and Bradford. Although traffic between Keighley and Bradford is now directed towards the A650 Bingley Relief Road, traffic in Main Street can still be busy. Keighley Jets Optare Solo No. 151 was pictured on a congested Main Street on 6 November 2021, working to Cullingworth, up above Bingley on the moors.

A photograph from Rochdale Road, Harpurhey, taken on 12 November 2021. Go North West No. 3105 heads into the centre of Manchester on service 18 from Langley, a large housing estate in Middleton. As a cursory glance will testify, the eastern suburbs of Manchester have undergone significant post-war redevelopment due to slum clearances and a rapid decline in population levels.

Goldthorpe is situated in the Barnsley district of South Yorkshire, an area once dominated by Yorkshire Traction. Today, Stagecoach dominates the transport scene following the takeover of the much missed 'Tracky'. In fading light, No. 28674 works through Goldthorpe on service X19.

A good, orderly, typically British queue had formed at Thurcroft for the Stagecoach East Midlands service to Worksop in Nottinghamshire. No. 15177 carries Aspire branding and is based at Worksop. Few Stagecoach buses were operating in South Yorkshire on 3 December 2021 due to an industrial dispute.

The Leigh-Salford-Manchester Bus Rapid Transit scheme began operation on 3 April 2016 at a cost of £122 million. Approaching Sale Lane, Tyldesley, is First No. 39252, a Volvo B5LH/Wright StreetDeck, resplendent in Vantage branding. This innovative route is a well patronised and interesting alternative to other modes of travel. Tyldesley is situated in the Wigan district of Greater Manchester.

Warrington's Own Buses, perhaps remarkably, continues as a municipal operator in 2021. Lancashire municipals such as Fylde, Hyndburn, Lancaster, Rossendale and more recently Halton have all ceased trading over the past few decades. Services from Warrington penetrate as far as Altrincham, Newton-le-Willows and Northwich. No. 312 was pictured departing Leigh for Warrington on a chilly 9 December 2021.

A lightly loaded Alexander Dennis Enviro400 works through Prescot on Arriva route 10A from St Helens to Liverpool. Several double-deckers work from St Helens depot in order to maximise potential loadings on this busy route. In Corporation and PTE days, St Helens traditionally had a higher allocation of single-deckers than most other Merseyside depots. Prescot, 9 December 2012.

The cracked glass of a vandalised bus shelter provides the frame for this view of Stagecoach No. 11111 at Ormskirk. Bringing up the rear is Gold-branded No. 15854. A popular market town, Ormskirk is home to Edge Hill University and is located around the West Lancashire Plain.

Herdings is located in the spectacularly hilly Gleadless Valley area of Sheffield. Large post-war estates stand on the lofty hills overlooking the city in what was once a rural idyll close to Derbyshire. First No. 63907 was pictured on the cross-city route to Chapeltown in late 2021.

Evening rush hour at Woodlands, Adwick-le-Street, in the company of First South Yorkshire No. 37103. A Volvo B9TL/Wright Eclipse Gemini, she was pictured on the Great North Road north of Doncaster. The nearby Woodlands Estate was an early example of a planned model estate. Dating from around 1910, the estate was built for the workers of Brodsworth Main Colliery.

A final picture from Thornley Station Industrial Estate near Shotton Colliery and Wheatley Hill in County Durham. In this snowy view are two of Garnett's double-deckers, usually used on school runs. On the left is Y508 NHK, a Dennis Trident new to Stagecoach East London. On the right is a fine Wright-bodied Volvo B7TL new to London General. Despite the east Durham location, Garnett's are based at Tindale Crescent near Bishop Auckland. Taken on January 2022.